HAL•LEONARD®
BASS
PLAY-ALONG

AUDIO
ACCESS
INCLUDED

BLUES

VOL. 9

PLAYBACK+
Speed • Pitch • Balance • Loop

To access audio visit:
www.halleonard.com/mylibrary

8623-9414-0540-8341

ISBN: 978-1-4234-1422-3

Visit Hal Leonard Online at www.halleonard.com

HAL•LEONARD®
7777 W. BLUEMOUND RD. P.O. BOX 13819
MILWAUKEE, WISCONSIN 53213

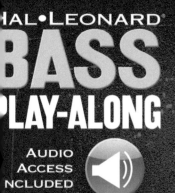

Hal•Leonard®
Bass
Play-Along

AUDIO
ACCESS
INCLUDED

VOL. 9

BLUES

CONTENTS

All Your Love
(I Miss Loving)

Words and Music by Otis Rush

Intro
Moderately ♩ = 128

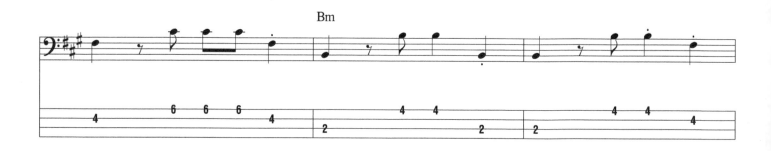

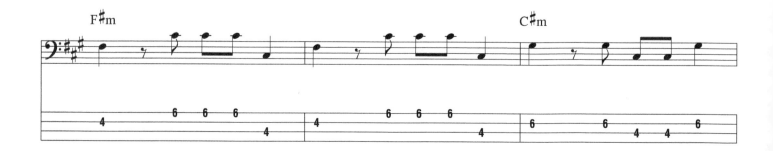

1. All the love I miss

Verse

2nd time, substitute Fill 1

lov - in',
all the kiss-es I miss kiss - in'.

2. See additional lyrics

All the love I miss lov - in', _____ all the kiss-es I miss

kiss - in'. _____ Be - fore I met you, ba - by,

Fill 1

I did-n't know what I was miss-in'. _____ 2. All the love, _____ pret-ty

I know you love me, too. _____

Interlude

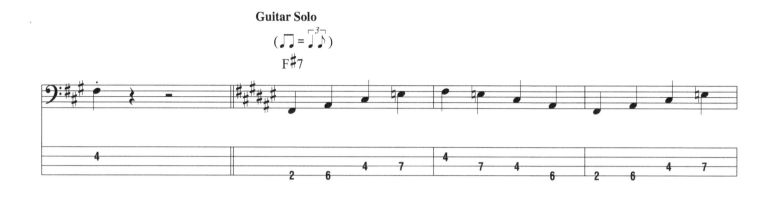

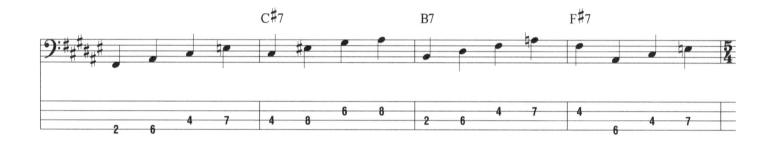

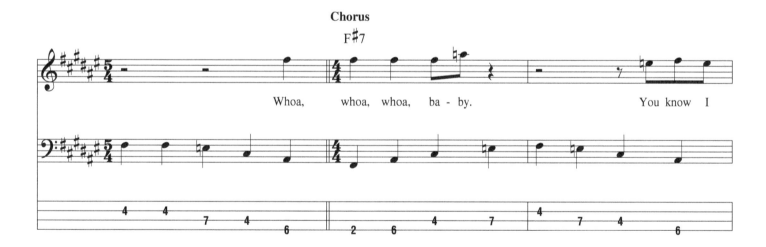

Chorus

Whoa, whoa, whoa, ba - by. You know I

love you, ba - by. Yeah, yeah, ba - by.

7

Additional Lyrics

2. All the love, pretty baby,
I have in store for you.
All the love, pretty baby,
I have in store for you.
The way I love you, baby,
I know you love me, too.

Born Under a Bad Sign

Words and Music by Booker T. Jones and William Bell

Intro
Moderate Blues ♩ = 92

Chorus

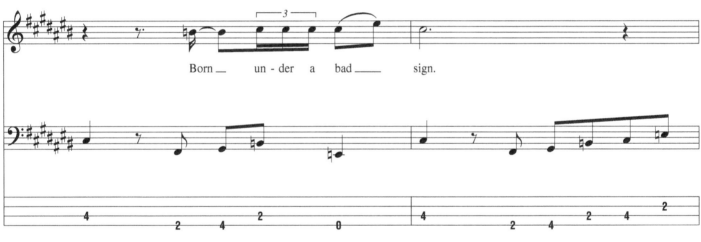

Born __ un - der a bad __ sign.

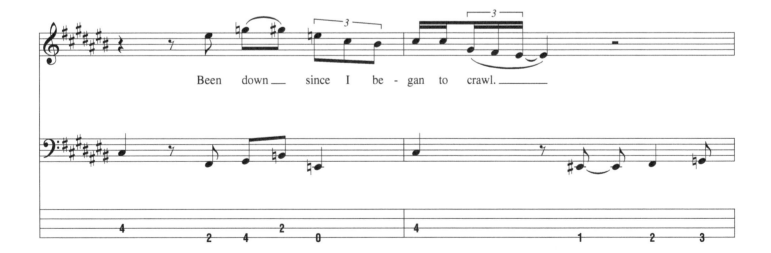

Been down __ since I be - gan to crawl. _____

9

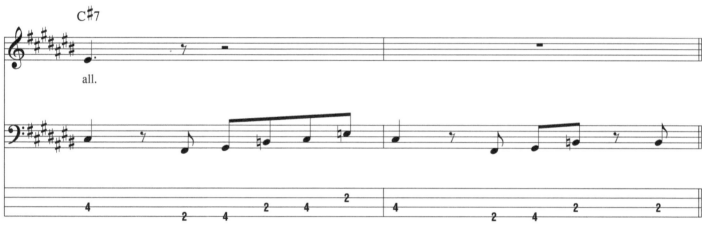

⊕ Coda

Additional Lyrics

2. I can't read, I didn't learn how to write.
   My whole life has been one big fight.

3. You know, wine and women is all I crave.
   A big leg woman gonna carry me to my grave.

I'm Your Hoochie Coochie Man

Written by Willie Dixon

Coda 1

ev - 'ry - bod - y____ knows I'm here. ____

Guitar Solo

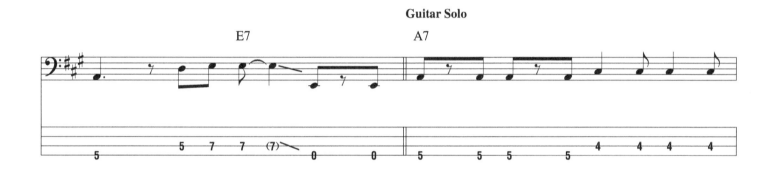

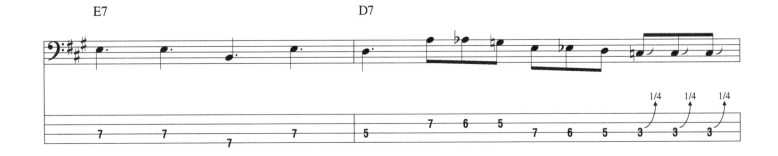

D.S. al Coda 2

$\oint$ **Coda 2**

Chorus

don't you mess with me. But you know I'm here. ____

Ev - 'ry - bod - y knows ____ I'm here. ____

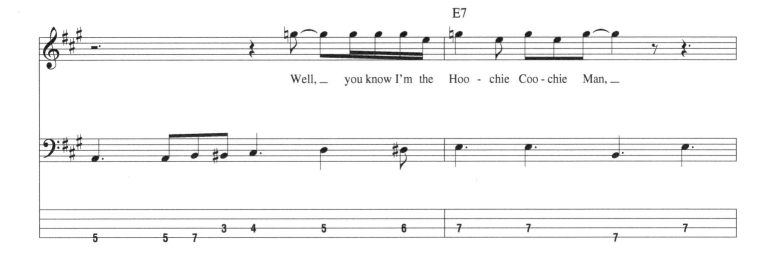

Well, __ you know I'm the Hoo - chie Coo - chie Man, __

the whole __ round __ world knows I'm here.

Additional Lyrics

2. I got a black cat bone,
   I got a mojo too.
   I got the John the Conquerroot,
   I'm gonna mess with you.
   I'm gonna make you girls
   Lead me by my hand.
   Then the world'll know
   I'm the Hoochie Coochie man.

3. On the seventh hour,
   On the seventh day,
   On the seventh month,
   The seventh doctor say,
   "You were born for good luck,
   And that you'll see."
   I got seven hundred dollars,
   Don't you mess with me.

I'm Tore Down

Words and Music by Sonny Thompson

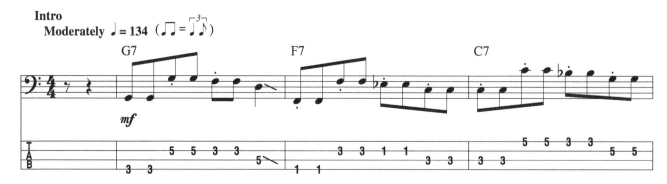

Chorus

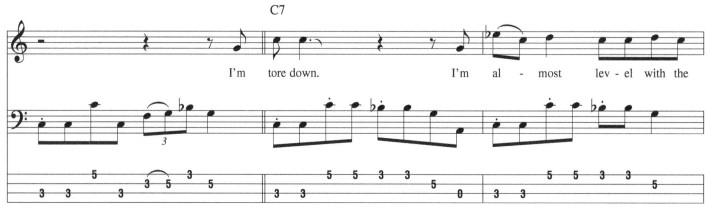

I'm tore down. I'm al-most lev-el with the

ground. _ I'm tore down. _ I'm

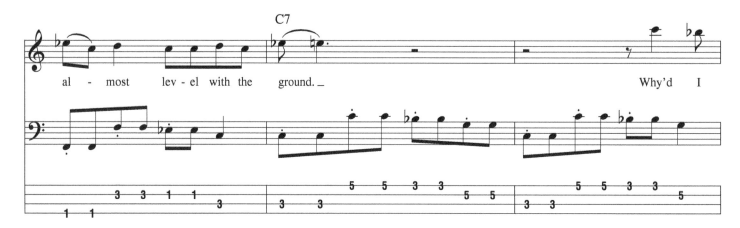

al-most lev-el with the ground. _ Why'd I

feel _ like this _ when _ my ba - by can't be found? _

Verse

1. Went to the riv - er, to jump in. My

Chorus

ba - by showed up and said, "I will tell you when." Well, I'm tore down,

al - most lev - el with the ground. _ Why'd _ I

feel _ like this _ when _ my ba - by can't be found? _

𝄋 Verse

2. I love you, babe, _ with all my heart _ and soul. _
3. *See additional lyrics*

2nd time, substitute Fill 1

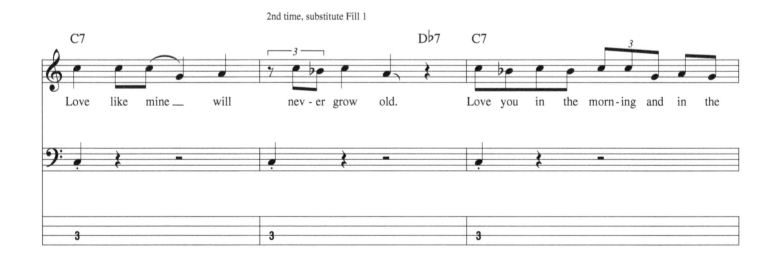

Love like mine _ will nev - er grow old. Love you in the morn-ing and in the

Fill 1

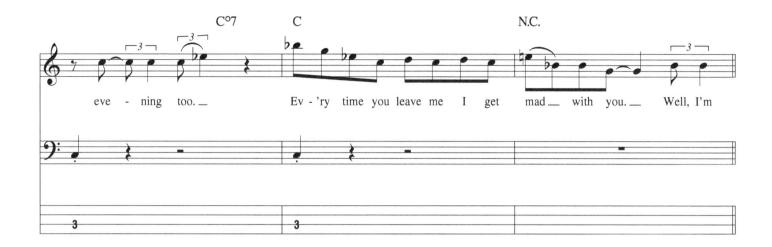

eve - ning too. Ev-'ry time you leave me I get mad with you. Well, I'm

Chorus

tore down. I'm al - most lev-el with the ground.

2nd time, substitute Fill 2

Why'd I feel like this when my

Fill 2

To Coda ⊕

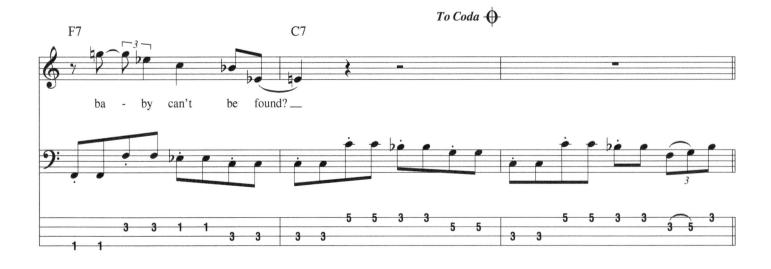

ba - by can't be found? __

Guitar Solo

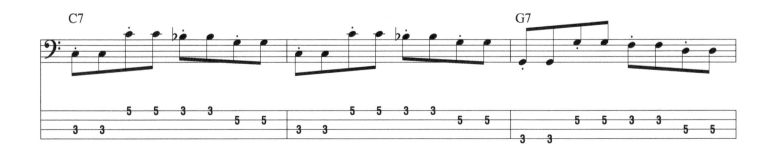

24

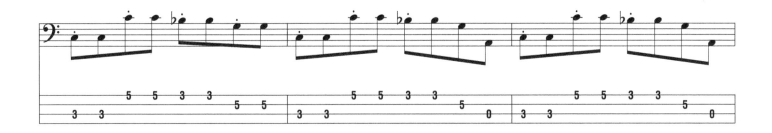

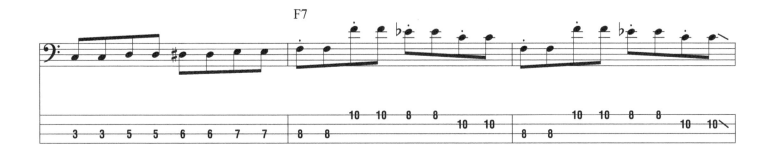

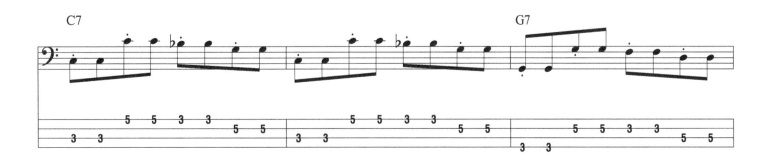

D.S. al Coda

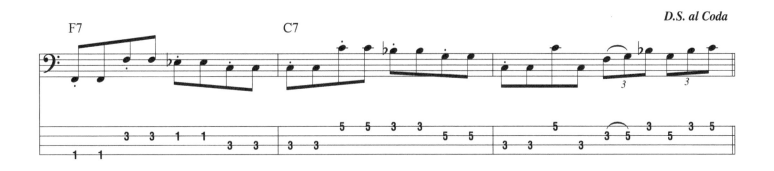

⊕ Coda

Outro-Chorus

C7

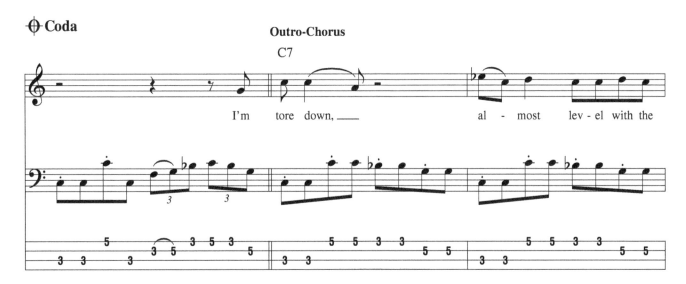

I'm   tore down, ____   al - most   lev - el with the

ground. _   Well, I'm   tore   down. _   I'm

al - most   lev - el   with the   ground. _   Why'd _   I

feel _ like this _ when _ my   ba - by can't be found? _

Additional Lyrics

3. Love you, baby, with all my might.
    Love like mine is outta sight.
    I'll lie for you if you want me to.
    I really don't believe that your love is true.

Killing Floor

Words and Music by Chester Burnett

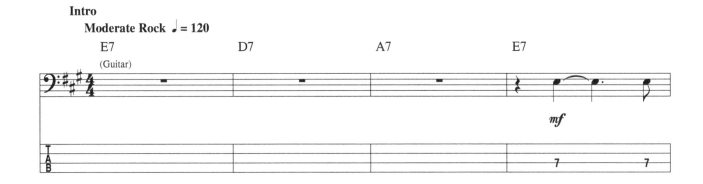

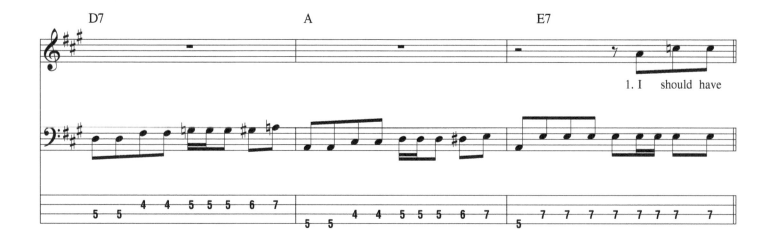

1. I should have

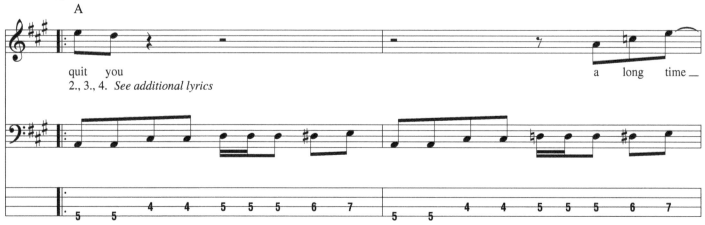

quit you

2., 3., 4. *See additional lyrics*

a long time __

__ a - go. __

I should have quit you, babe,

4th time, To Coda ⊕

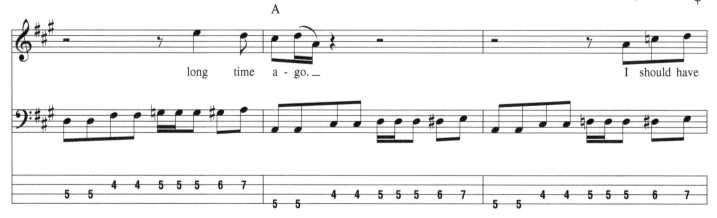

long time a - go. __

I should have

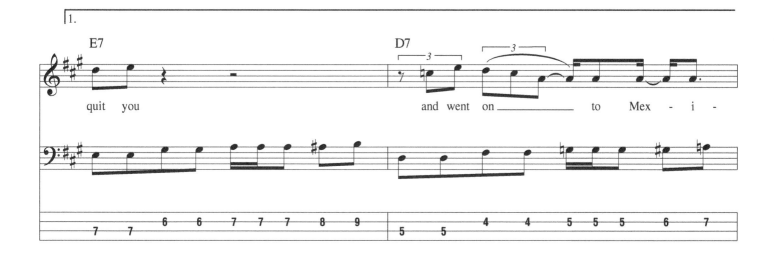

quit you

and went on _____ to Mex - i -

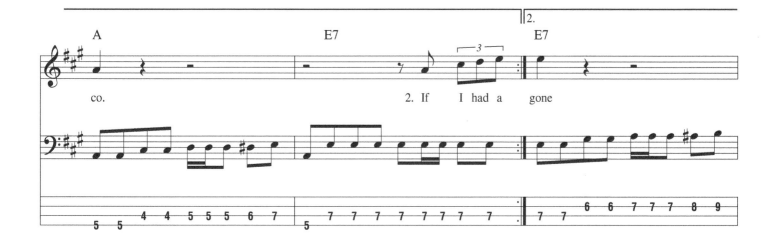

co.

2. If I had a gone

since my ___ sec - ond time. ___

Guitar Solo

A

D.S. al Coda
(take repeat)

3. I   should have

 Coda

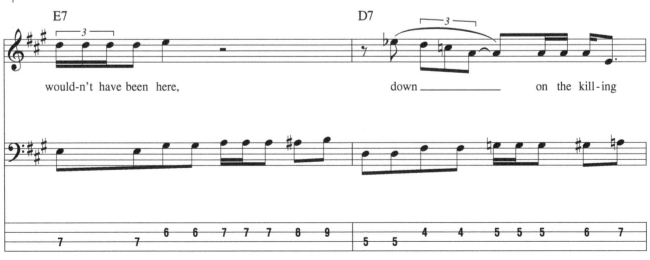

would-n't have been here,   down _____ on the kill-ing

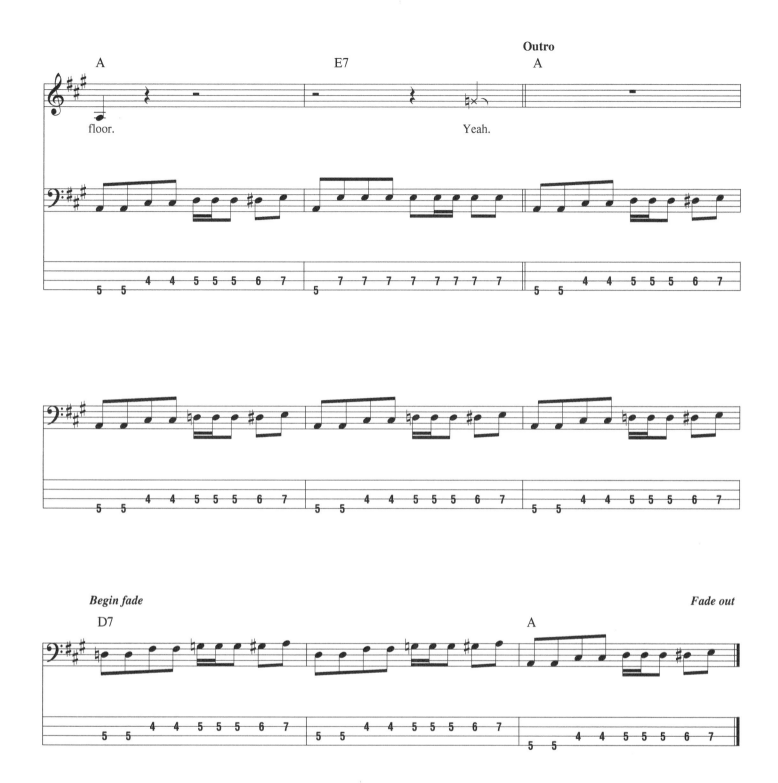

Additional Lyrics

2. If I had a followed my first mind,
   If I had a followed my first mind,
   I'd a been gone since my second time.

3. I should have went on when my friend come from Mexico at me.
   I should have went on when my friend come from Mexico at me.
   But now I'm foolin' with you, baby, I let you put me on the killing floor.

4. God knows I should have been gone.
   God knows I should have been gone.
   Then I wouldn't have been here, down on the killing floor.

Sweet Home Chicago

Words and Music by Robert Johnson

back _ to that same old _ place, _ sweet home _ Chi -

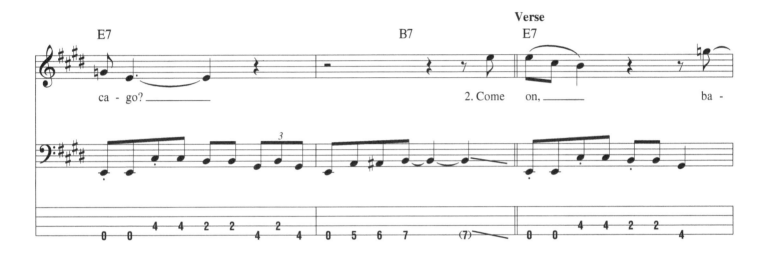

ca - go? _____ 2. Come on, _____ ba -

- by, don't-cha wan - na go? _____ Come on, _

ba - by, don't-cha wan - na go _____

back __ to that same old __ place, __   sweet home __ Chi -

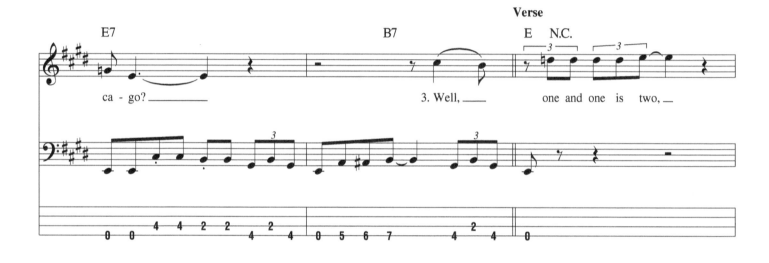

Verse

ca - go? _____   3. Well, ____   one and one is two, __

six and two is eight. __   Come on, __ ba - by, don't-cha make me late. ___

Hey,   ba - by, don't-cha wan - na go _____

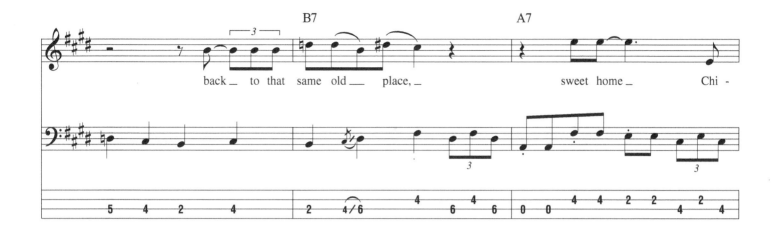

back __ to that same old __ place, __ sweet home __ Chi-

ca - go? _____ 4. Come on, _____ ba-

- by, don't-cha wan - na go? _____ Come on, __

ba - by, don't-cha wan - na go _____

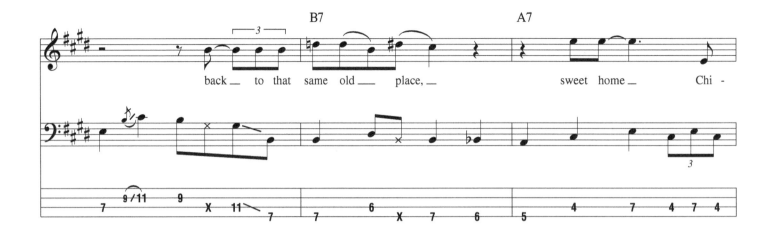

back — to that same old — place, — sweet home — Chi -

Guitar Solo

ca - go? ——

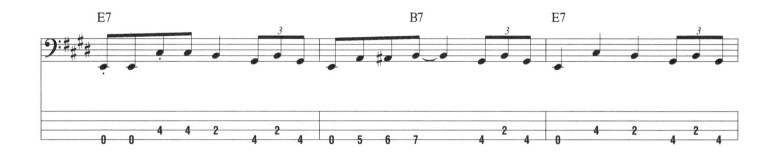

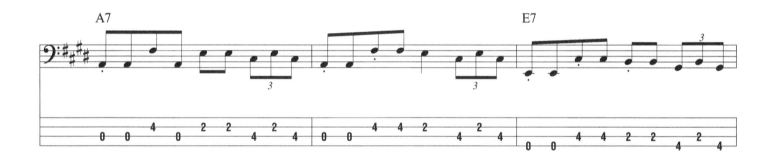

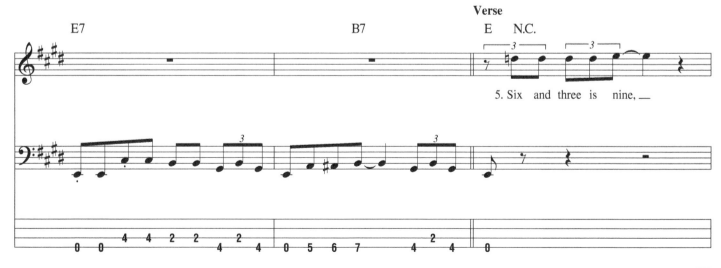

5. Six and three is nine, ___

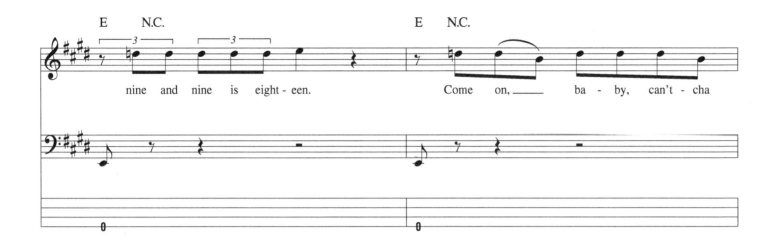

nine and nine is eight - een. Come on, _____ ba - by, can't - cha

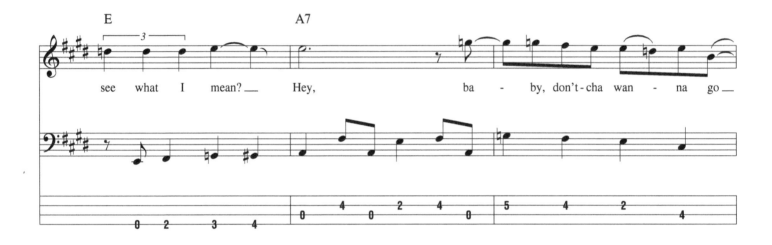

see what I mean? _____ Hey, ba - by, don't - cha wan - na go _____

back _____ to that same old _____ place, _____

sweet home _____ Chi - ca - go? _____ 6. Ah, come on, _____

ba - by, don't you __ wan - na go? ____

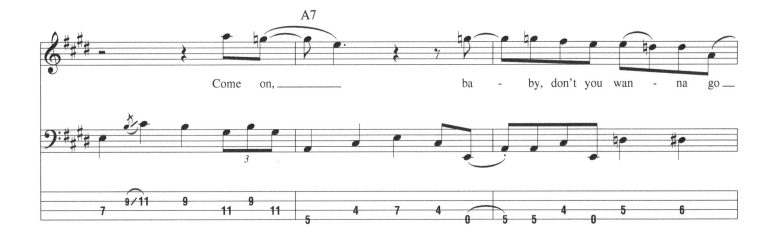

Come on, ____ ba - by, don't you wan - na go __

back __ to that same old __ place, __

sweet home __ Chi - ca - go? ____

Pride and Joy

Written by Stevie Ray Vaughan

Tune down 1/2 step:
(low to high) Eb-Ab-Db-Gb

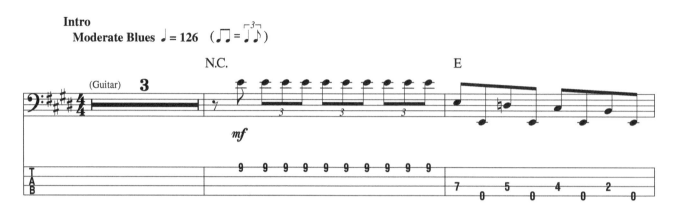

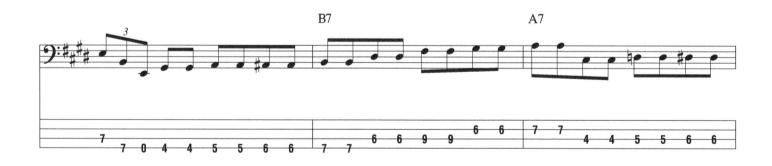

Verse

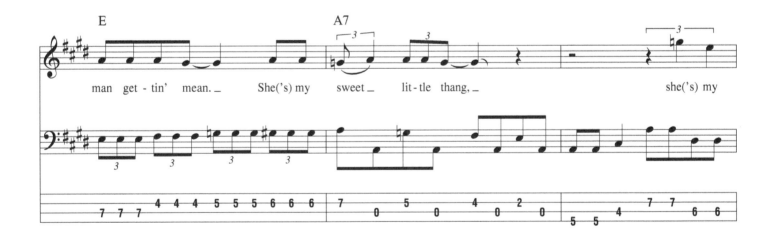

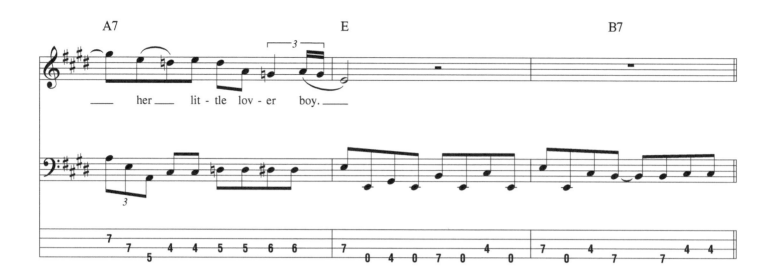

her ___ lit - tle lov - er boy. ___

Guitar Solo

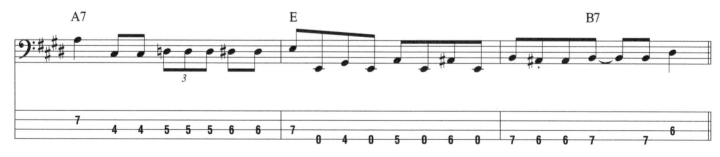

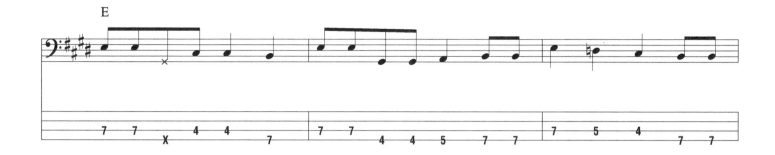

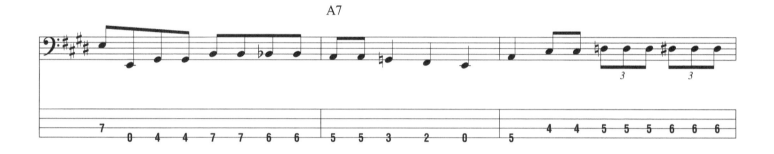

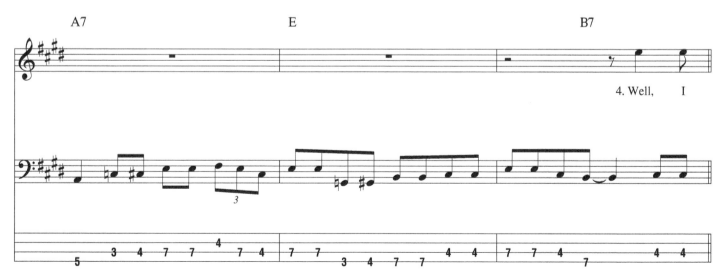

4. Well, I

Verse

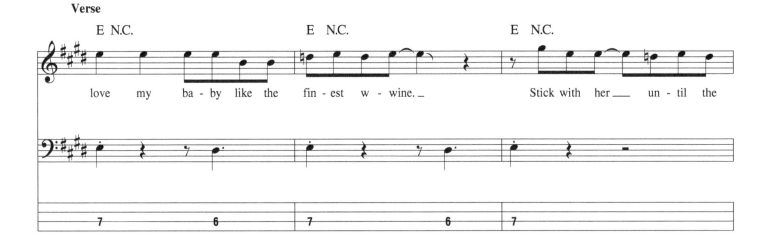

love my ba - by like the fin - est w - wine. __ Stick with her __ un - til the

end of time. __ An' she('s) my sweet __ lit - tle thang, __ she('s) my

pride and joy. __ She('s) my sweet lit - tle ba - by, I'm __

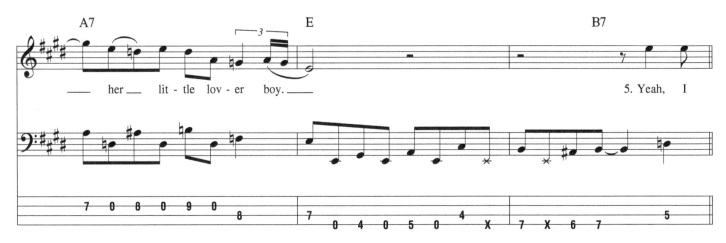

__ her __ lit - tle lov - er boy. __ 5. Yeah, I

Verse

love my ba - by, my heart and ___ soul. ___ Love like ___ ours, ah, won't ___

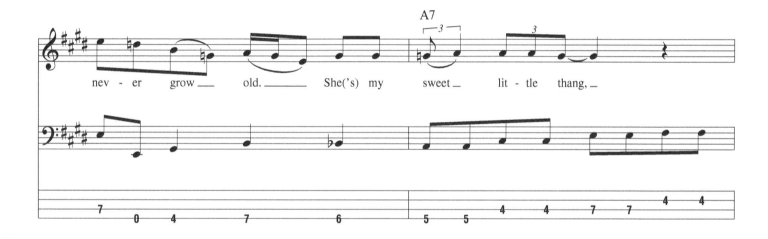

nev - er grow ___ old. _____ She('s) my sweet ___ lit - tle thang, ___

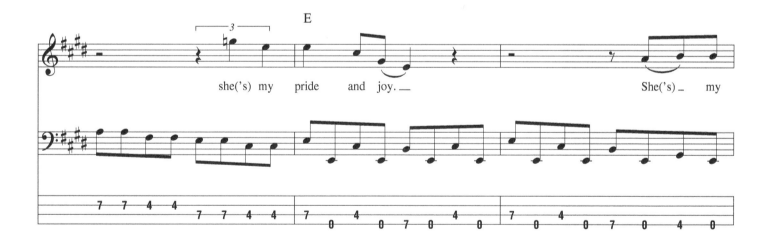

she('s) my pride and joy. ___ She('s) ___ my

sweet lit - tle ba - by, I'm ___ her ___ lit - tle lov - er boy. ___

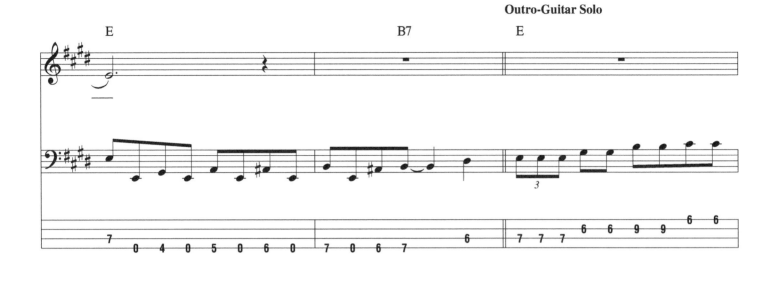

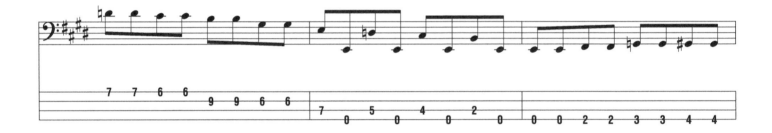

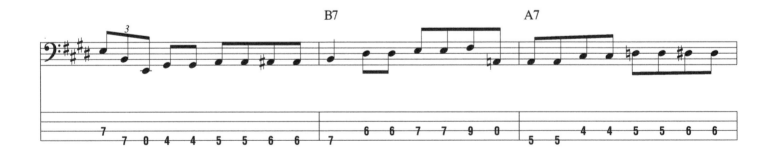

The Thrill Is Gone

Words and Music by Roy Hawkins and Rick Darnell

Verse

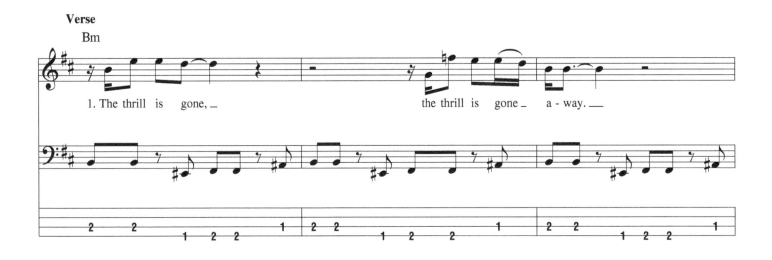

1. The thrill is gone, ___ the thrill is gone ___ a - way. ___

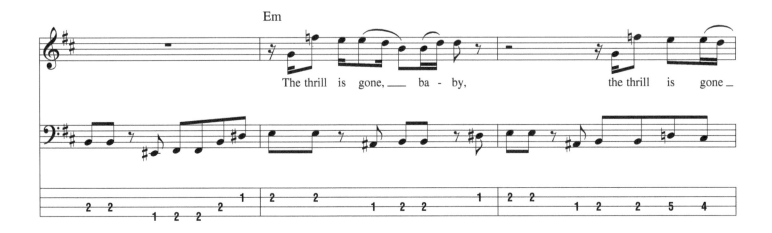

The thrill is gone, ___ ba - by, the thrill is gone ___

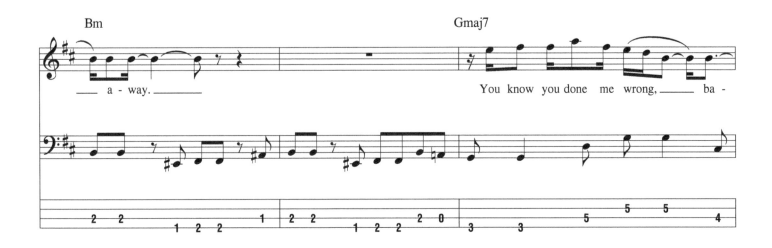

___ a - way. ___ You know you done me wrong, ___ ba -

- by, and you'll ___ be sor - ry some day. ___

Verse

2. The thrill is gone, it's gone a-way __ from me. __

The thrill is gone, __ ba - by, the thrill has

gone a - way __ from me. __ Al - though I'll __ still live on, __

but so __ lone - ly __ I'll __ be.

Guitar Solo

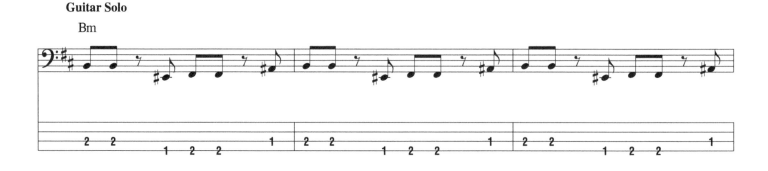

Verse

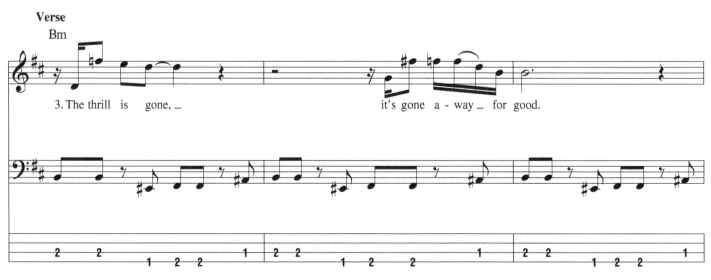

3. The thrill is gone, __ it's gone a - way __ for good.

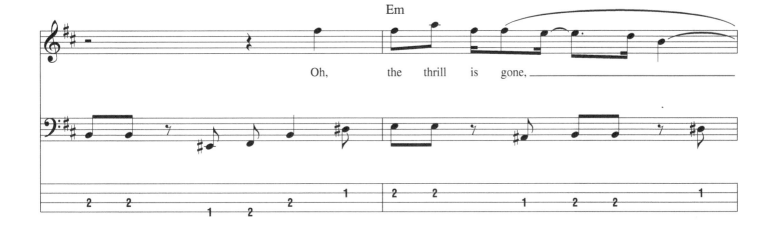

Oh, the thrill is gone,

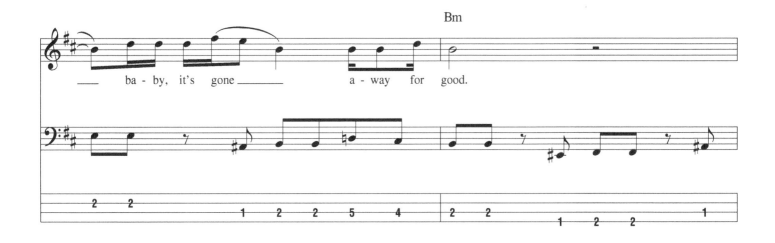

ba - by, it's gone _____ a - way for good.

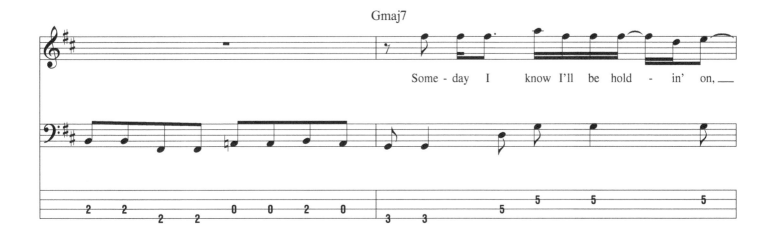

Some - day I know I'll be hold - in' on, _____

ba - by, just like I know _____ a good man _____ should.

Verse

Bm

4. You know I'm ___ free, free now, ___ ba - by, I'm free ___ from your ___ spell.

Em

Whoa, I'm free, ___ free, free ___ now, I'm free ___

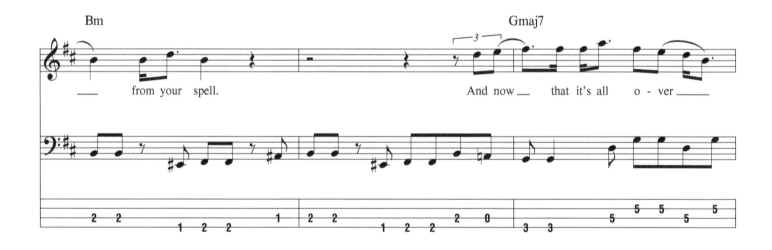

Bm   **Gmaj7**

___ from your spell. And now ___ that it's all o - ver ___

F#7   **Bm**

all I can do ___ is wish you ___ well. ___

Outro-Guitar Solo

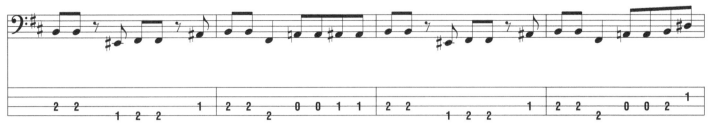

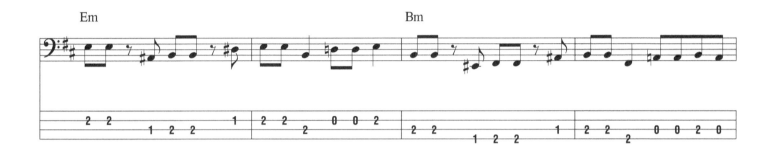

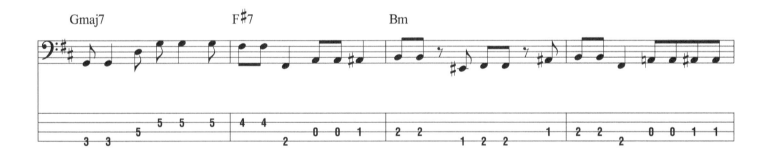

Repeat and fade

Play 9 times

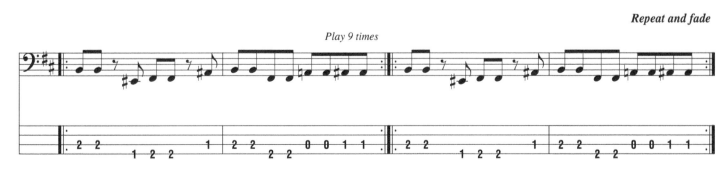

Bass Notation Legend

Bass music can be notated two different ways: on a *musical staff*, and in *tablature*

THE MUSICAL STAFF shows pitches and rhythms and is divided by bar lines into measures. Pitches are named after the first seven letters of the alphabet.

TABLATURE graphically represents the bass fingerboard. Each horizontal line represents a string, and each number represents a fret.

Notes:

Strings:

3rd string, open — 2nd string, 2nd fret — 1st & 2nd strings open, played together

HAMMER-ON: Strike the first (lower) note with one finger, then sound the higher note (on the same string) with another finger by fretting it without picking.

PULL-OFF: Place both fingers on the notes to be sounded. Strike the first note and without picking, pull the finger off to sound the second (lower) note.

LEGATO SLIDE: Strike the first note and then slide the same fret-hand finger up or down to the second note. The second note is not struck.

SHIFT SLIDE: Same as legato slide, except the second note is struck.

TRILL: Very rapidly alternate between the notes indicated by continuously hammering on and pulling off.

TREMOLO PICKING: The note is picked as rapidly and continuously as possible.

VIBRATO: The string is vibrated by rapidly bending and releasing the note with the fretting hand.

SHAKE: Using one finger, rapidly alternate between two notes on one string by sliding either a half-step above or below.

NATURAL HARMONIC: Strike the note while the fret hand lightly touches the string directly over the fret indicated.

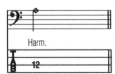

MUFFLED STRINGS: A percussive sound is produced by laying the fret hand across the string(s) without depressing them and striking them with the pick hand.

BEND: Strike the note and bend up the interval shown.

BEND AND RELEASE: Strike the note and bend up as indicated, then release back to the original note. Only the first note is struck.

RIGHT-HAND TAP: Hammer ("tap") the fret indicated with the "pick-hand" index or middle finger and pull off to the note fretted by the fret hand.

LEFT-HAND TAP: Hammer ("tap") the fret indicated with the "fret-hand" index or middle finger.

SLAP: Strike ("slap") string with right-hand thumb.

POP: Snap ("pop") string with right-hand index or middle finger.

Additional Musical Definitions

 (accent) • Accentuate note (play it louder)

 (accent) • Accentuate note with great intensity

 (staccato) • Play the note short

D.S. al Coda • Go back to the sign (𝄋), then play until the measure marked ***"To Coda"***, then skip to the section labelled ***"Coda."***

Fill • Label used to identify a brief pattern which is to be inserted into the arrangement.

• Repeat measures between signs.

1. 2. • When a repeated section has different endings, play the first ending only the first time and the second ending only the second time.